FOR THE BEST SISTER EVER

FOR THE BEST SISTER EVER

This edition copyright © Octopus Publishing Group Limited, 2026
First published in 2015 as *For the Best Sister in the World*

All rights reserved.

No part of this book may be reproduced by any means, nor transmitted, nor translated into a machine language, without the written permission of the publishers.

Condition of Sale
This book is sold subject to the condition that it shall not, by way of trade or otherwise, be lent, resold, hired out or otherwise circulated in any form of binding or cover other than that in which it is published and without a similar condition including this condition being imposed on the subsequent purchaser.

An Hachette UK Company
www.hachette.co.uk

Summersdale Publishers
Part of Octopus Publishing Group Limited
Carmelite House
50 Victoria Embankment
LONDON
EC4Y 0DZ
UK

This FSC® label means that materials and other controlled sources used for the product have been responsibly sourced

www.summersdale.com

The authorized representative in the EEA is Hachette Ireland, 8 Castlecourt Centre, Dublin 15, D15 XTP3, Ireland (email: info@hbgi.ie)

Printed and bound in China

ISBN: 978-1-83799-835-7
eISBN: 978-1-78783-439-2

Substantial discounts on bulk quantities of Summersdale books are available to corporations, professional associations and other organizations. For details contact general enquiries: telephone: +44 (0) 1243 771107 or email: enquiries@summersdale.com.

TO..........................

FROM...................

IS SOLACE ANYWHERE MORE
COMFORTING THAN THAT IN
THE ARMS OF A SISTER?

Alice Walker

WHATEVER YOU DO THEY WILL LOVE YOU.

Deborah Moggach

THE BOND THAT LINKS YOUR TRUE FAMILY IS NOT ONE OF BLOOD, BUT OF RESPECT AND JOY IN EACH OTHER'S LIFE.

RICHARD BACH

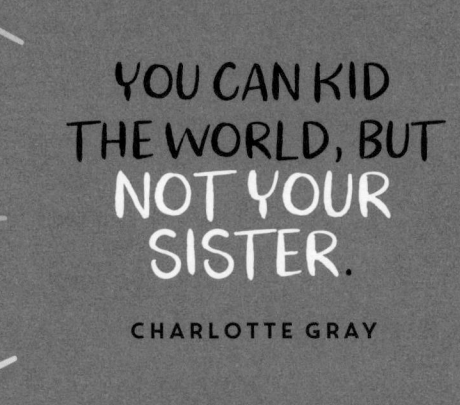

FRIENDS MAY COME AND GO, BUT SISTERS ARE FOREVER

I SUSTAIN MYSELF WITH THE LOVE OF FAMILY.

MAYA ANGELOU

All women are naturally badass.

Alicia Keys

> "A FAMILY IS A UNIT COMPOSED NOT ONLY OF CHILDREN BUT OF MEN, WOMEN, AN OCCASIONAL ANIMAL, AND THE COMMON COLD."
>
> Ogden Nash

HELPING ONE ANOTHER IS PART OF THE RELIGION OF OUR SISTERHOOD.

LOUISA MAY ALCOTT

KNOWING
I HAVE A **SISTER**,
I KNOW I ALWAYS
HAVE A **FRIEND**

ARE WE NOT LIKE TWO VOLUMES OF ONE BOOK?

Marceline Desbordes-Valmore

FOLLOW YOUR OWN STAR.

DANTE ALIGHIERI

IN THEE MY SOUL SHALL
HOLD COMBINED
THE SISTER AND THE FRIEND.

Catherine Killigrew

BROTHERS AND SISTERS ARE AS CLOSE AS HANDS AND FEET.

Vietnamese proverb

A HAPPY FAMILY IS BUT AN EARLIER HEAVEN.

GEORGE BERNARD SHAW

CHILDREN OF THE SAME FAMILY, THE SAME BLOOD, WITH THE SAME FIRST ASSOCIATIONS AND HABITS, HAVE SOME MEANS OF ENJOYMENT IN THEIR POWER, WHICH NO SUBSEQUENT CONNECTIONS CAN SUPPLY.

Jane Austen

> **THERE IS NO LIMIT TO WHAT WE, AS WOMEN, CAN ACCOMPLISH.**
>
> Michelle Obama

REJOICE WITH YOUR FAMILY IN THE BEAUTIFUL LAND OF LIFE!

ALBERT EINSTEIN

Sister is probably the most competitive relationship within the family, but once the sisters are grown, it becomes the strongest relationship.

Margaret Mead

YOU BRING

OUT MY

INNER CHILD

> **BLESS YOU, MY DARLING, AND REMEMBER YOU ARE ALWAYS IN THE HEART... OF YOUR SISTER.**
>
> KATHERINE MANSFIELD

A SISTER CAN BE SEEN AS
SOMEONE WHO IS BOTH
OURSELVES AND VERY MUCH
NOT OURSELVES — A SPECIAL
KIND OF DOUBLE.

Toni Morrison

> YOU DON'T CHOOSE YOUR FAMILY. THEY ARE GOD'S GIFT TO YOU, AS YOU ARE TO THEM.
>
> Desmond Tutu

OTHER THINGS MAY
CHANGE US, BUT WE
START AND END
WITH FAMILY.

Anthony Brandt

MORE THAN SANTA CLAUS, YOUR SISTER KNOWS WHEN YOU'VE BEEN **BAD AND GOOD.**

LINDA SUNSHINE

OUR ROOTS SAY WE'RE **SISTERS**, OUR HEARTS SAY WE'RE **FRIENDS**

SISTERLY LOVE IS, OF ALL SENTIMENTS, THE MOST ABSTRACT.

UGO BETTI

Every family has a story that it tells itself, that it passes on to the children and grandchildren. The story grows over the years... it becomes the flagpole that the family hangs its identity from.

A. M. Homes

> "NO ONE CAN MAKE YOU FEEL INFERIOR WITHOUT YOUR CONSENT."
>
> Eleanor Roosevelt

FAMILY IS WHAT GROUNDS YOU.

ANGELINA JOLIE

There can be no situation in life in which the conversation of my dear sister will not administer some comfort to me.

Mary Wortley Montagu

WHEN SISTERS STAND SHOULDER TO SHOULDER, WHO STANDS A CHANCE AGAINST US?

PAM BROWN

. YOU CAN KISS YOUR FAMILY AND FRIENDS GOODBYE AND PUT MILES BETWEEN YOU, BUT AT THE SAME TIME YOU CARRY THEM WITH YOU IN YOUR HEART.

Frederick Buechner

YOU ALWAYS KNOW THE RIGHT THING TO SAY, EVEN IF IT'S NOT WHAT I WANT TO HEAR!

A SISTER IS BOTH
YOUR MIRROR –
AND YOUR OPPOSITE.

Elizabeth Fishel

> "MOST ARE LIKE MY SISTER AND ME... LINKED BY VOLATILE LOVE, BEST FRIENDS WHO MAKE OTHER BEST FRIENDS EVER SO SLIGHTLY LESS BEST.
>
> Patricia Volk

I, WHO HAVE NO SISTERS OR BROTHERS, LOOK WITH SOME DEGREE OF INNOCENT ENVY ON THOSE WHO MAY BE SAID TO BE BORN TO FRIENDS.

JAMES BOSWELL

> THE FAMILY –
> THAT DEAR OCTOPUS FROM WHOSE TENTACLES WE NEVER QUITE ESCAPE, NOR, IN OUR INMOST HEARTS, EVER QUITE WISH TO.
>
> DODIE SMITH

A SISTER IS A
FOREVER FRIEND

> SISTERS FUNCTION AS SAFETY NETS IN A CHAOTIC WORLD SIMPLY BY BEING THERE FOR EACH OTHER.
>
> Carol Saline

"

SWEET IS THE VOICE
OF A SISTER IN THE
SEASON OF SORROW,
AND WISE IS THE
COUNSEL OF THOSE
WHO LOVE US.

Benjamin Disraeli

"

BEING YOURSELF AND BEING TRUE TO WHAT MAKES YOU HAPPY IS THE MOST **IMPORTANT THING.**

ZOOEY DESCHANEL

Because there's one thing stronger than magic: sisterhood.

Robin Benway

IF YOU LOOK DEEPLY INTO THE PALM OF YOUR HAND, YOU WILL SEE YOUR PARENTS AND ALL GENERATIONS OF YOUR ANCESTORS. ALL OF THEM ARE ALIVE IN THIS MOMENT. EACH IS PRESENT IN YOUR BODY.

THÍCH NHẤT HẠNH

A SISTER SHARES CHILDHOOD MEMORIES AND GROWN-UP DREAMS

THE FAMILY IS THE COUNTRY OF THE HEART.

Giuseppe Mazzini

"YOU KNOW FULL WELL AS I DO THE VALUE OF SISTERS' AFFECTIONS: THERE IS NOTHING LIKE IT IN THIS WORLD.

Charlotte Brontë

IN TIME OF TEST, FAMILY IS BEST.

Burmese proverb

THERE IS NO BETTER FRIEND THAN A SISTER. AND THERE IS NO BETTER SISTER THAN YOU.

ANONYMOUS

HAVING A SISTER MEANS ALWAYS HAVING BACKUP

FOLLOW YOUR INNER MOONLIGHT; DON'T HIDE THE MADNESS.

ALLEN GINSBERG

I DON'T BELIEVE AN ACCIDENT OF BIRTH MAKES PEOPLE SISTERS OR BROTHERS. SISTERHOOD AND BROTHERHOOD IS A CONDITION PEOPLE HAVE TO WORK AT.

Maya Angelou

> WOMEN SPEAKING UP FOR THEMSELVES AND FOR THOSE AROUND THEM IS THE STRONGEST FORCE WE HAVE TO CHANGE THE WORLD.

Melinda Gates

FAMILY COMES FIRST. YOU'RE THE ONLY THING THEY HAVE.

HEIDI KLUM

SOMEONE TO LEAN ON, SOMEONE TO COUNT ON... SOMEONE TO TELL ON!

A sister smiles when one tells one's stories – for she knows where the decoration has been added.

Chris Montaigne

BE
UNAPOLOGETICALLY
YOU.

Steve Maraboli

SISTERHOOD IS POWERFUL.

ROBIN MORGAN

SISTER IS OUR FIRST FRIEND AND SECOND MOTHER.

Sunny Gupta

> **SISTERS ARE THERE WITH US FROM THE DAWN OF OUR PERSONAL STORIES TO THE INEVITABLE DUSK.**
>
> Susan Scarf Merrell

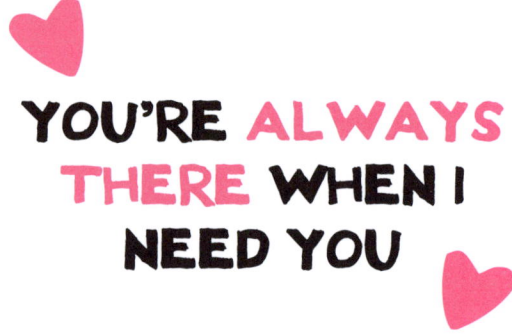

> WE ACQUIRE FRIENDS AND WE MAKE ENEMIES, BUT OUR SISTERS COME WITH THE TERRITORY.
>
> **EVELYN LOEB**

> YOU KEEP YOUR PAST BY HAVING SISTERS... THEY'RE THE ONLY ONES WHO DON'T GET BORED IF YOU TALK ABOUT YOUR MEMORIES.
>
> Deborah Moggach

WE MAY LOOK OLD AND WISE TO THE OUTSIDE WORLD. BUT TO EACH OTHER, WE ARE STILL IN JUNIOR SCHOOL.

CHARLOTTE GRAY

FAMILY LIFE IS TOO INTIMATE TO BE PRESERVED BY THE SPIRIT OF JUSTICE. IT CAN BE SUSTAINED BY A SPIRIT OF LOVE.

REINHOLD NIEBUHR

YOU ARE

THE BEST!

> **SOMEONE WHO SEES YOU EXACTLY AS YOU ARE, AND THINKS THAT IS ENOUGH.**
>
> Barbara Bush on her sister

Never doubt that you are valuable and powerful and deserving of every chance and opportunity in the world.

Hillary Clinton

WE HAVE BEEN BANDED TOGETHER UNDER PACK CODES AND TRIBAL LAWS.

Rose Macaulay

FOR THERE IS NO FRIEND LIKE A SISTER, IN CALM OR STORMY WEATHER.

CHRISTINA ROSSETTI

IN THE **COOKIES** OF LIFE, SISTERS ARE THE **CHOCOLATE** CHIPS

WHAT SETS SISTERS APART FROM BROTHERS AND ALSO FROM FRIENDS IS A VERY INTIMATE MESHING OF HEART, SOUL AND THE MYSTICAL CORDS OF MEMORY.

Carol Saline

FAMILIES ARE THE
COMPASS THAT
GUIDE US.

BRAD HENRY

"EVERY WOMAN HAS THE RIGHT TO BECOME HERSELF, AND DO WHATEVER SHE NEEDS TO DO.

Ani DiFranco

OUR SISTERS HOLD UP OUR MIRRORS: OUR IMAGES OF WHO WE ARE AND WHO WE CAN DARE TO BECOME.

ELIZABETH FISHEL

OUR DAYS OUT

TOGETHER

ARE THE

MOST FUN!

AN OLDER SISTER IS A FRIEND
AND DEFENDER — A LISTENER,
CONSPIRATOR, A COUNSELLOR
AND A SHARER OF DELIGHTS.
AND SORROWS TOO.

Pam Brown

IF WE ARE UNITED, THERE IS NO LIMIT TO WHAT WE CAN DO.

AMAL CLOONEY

Oh... the inexpressible comfort of feeling safe with a person; having neither to weigh thoughts nor measure words, but to pour them all out, just as they are.

Dinah Maria Craik

> "YOU HAVE TO BE UNIQUE, AND DIFFERENT, AND SHINE IN YOUR OWN WAY."
>
> Lady Gaga

THERE IS SPACE WITHIN SISTERHOOD FOR LIKENESS AND DIFFERENCE, FOR THE SUBTLE DIFFERENCES THAT CHALLENGE AND DELIGHT... AND SURPRISE.

CHRISTINE DOWNING

SO WE GREW TOGETHER,
LIKE TO A DOUBLE CHERRY,
SEEMING PARTED,
BUT YET AN UNION IN PARTITION;
TWO LOVELY BERRIES MOULDED
ON ONE STEM.

William Shakespeare

> **SISTERHOOD... IS, LIKE MOTHERHOOD, A CAPACITY, NOT A DESTINY. IT MUST BE CHOSEN, EXERCISED BY ACTS OF WILL.**
>
> Olga Broumas

A SISTER WILL ALWAYS UNDERSTAND

YOU ARE VALUED, YOU ARE A GODDESS AND DON'T FORGET THAT.

Jennifer Lopez

MAY YOU LIVE EVERY DAY OF YOUR LIFE.

JONATHAN SWIFT

THE LOVE OF FAMILY AND THE ADMIRATION OF FRIENDS IS MUCH MORE IMPORTANT THAN WEALTH AND PRIVILEGE.

CHARLES KURALT

> THE FAMILY IS OUR REFUGE AND OUR SPRINGBOARD; NOURISHED ON IT, WE CAN ADVANCE TO NEW HORIZONS.
>
> Alex Haley

A **TRUE** SISTER IS A FRIEND WHO **LISTENS** WITH HER HEART

> **BE YOURSELF. DO WHATEVER YOU WANT TO DO AND DON'T LET BOUNDARIES HOLD YOU BACK.**
>
> Sophie Turner

My sister accommodates me... She accepts and loves me, despite our differences.

Joy Harjo

MY FIRST JOB IS BIG SISTER AND I TAKE THAT VERY SERIOUSLY.

VENUS WILLIAMS

AN OUNCE OF BLOOD IS WORTH MORE THAN A POUND OF FRIENDSHIP.

Spanish proverb

IF I COULD
CHOOSE
MY FAMILY,
I'D STILL
CHOOSE YOU

FAMILY: LIKE BRANCHES ON A TREE, WE ALL GROW IN DIFFERENT DIRECTIONS, YET OUR ROOTS REMAIN AS ONE.

Anonymous

MY SIBLINGS ARE MY BEST FRIENDS.

America Ferrera

BIG SISTERS ARE THE CRAB GRASS IN THE LAWN OF LIFE.

CHARLES M. SCHULZ

A FAMILY NEEDS TO **WORK AS A TEAM**, SUPPORTING EACH OTHER'S INDIVIDUAL AIMS AND ASPIRATIONS.

BUZZ ALDRIN

> SHE'S MY LITTLE SISTER.
> MINE TO TORTURE AND
> MINE TO PROTECT.
>
> Julia Quinn

A MINISTERING ANGEL SHALL MY SISTER BE.

WILLIAM SHAKESPEARE

> **A GIRL SHOULD BE TWO THINGS: WHO AND WHAT SHE WANTS.**
>
> Coco Chanel

THE FAMILY IS ONE OF NATURE'S MASTERPIECES.

GEORGE SANTAYANA

**Just be yourself,
there is no one better.**

Taylor Swift

ONE REFUSING A SIBLING'S ADVICE BREAKS HIS ARM.

Somali proverb

I KNOW OUR FIGHTS WILL NEVER LAST

YOUR PARENTS LEAVE YOU TOO SOON AND YOUR KIDS AND SPOUSE COME ALONG LATE, BUT YOUR SIBLINGS KNOW YOU WHEN YOU ARE IN YOUR MOST INCHOATE FORM.

Jeffrey Kluger

> **TO US, FAMILY MEANS PUTTING YOUR ARMS AROUND EACH OTHER AND BEING THERE.**
>
> Barbara Bush

WE HAVE TO DARE TO BE OURSELVES, HOWEVER FRIGHTENING OR STRANGE THAT SELF MAY PROVE TO BE.

MAY SARTON

A FAMILY IN HARMONY WILL PROSPER IN EVERYTHING.

CHINESE PROVERB

THERE IS NO DOUBT THAT IT IS AROUND THE FAMILY AND THE HOME THAT ALL THE GREATEST VIRTUES… ARE CREATED, STRENGTHENED AND MAINTAINED.

Winston Churchill

I'M **SMILING** BECAUSE YOU'RE MY SISTER. I'M **LAUGHING** BECAUSE THERE'S **NOTHING** YOU CAN DO ABOUT IT!

> FAMILIES ARE THE BEST PLACE TO LEARN AND PRACTISE MUTUAL TOLERANCE AND ACCEPTANCE.
>
> BEGUM AGA KHAN

> Siblings: children of the same parents, each of whom is perfectly normal until they get together.
>
> Sam Levenson

THE ONLY ROCK I KNOW THAT STAYS STEADY, THE ONLY INSTITUTION I KNOW THAT WORKS, IS THE FAMILY.

LEE IACOCCA

Family faces are magic mirrors. Looking at people who belong to us, we see the past, present, and future.

Gail Lumet Buckley

YOU'RE BEAUTIFUL AND WORTHY AND TOTALLY UNIQUE.

Emma Stone

SISTERS ARE FOR SHARING LAUGHTER AND WIPING TEARS

THERE IS GREAT COMFORT
AND INSPIRATION IN THE
FEELING OF CLOSE HUMAN
RELATIONSHIPS.

Walt Disney

> "YOU ARE PERFECTLY CAST IN YOUR LIFE. I CAN'T IMAGINE ANYONE BUT YOU IN THE ROLE. GO PLAY."
>
> Lin-Manuel Miranda

A YOUNG LADY'S MOST NATURAL ALLY IS HER SISTER.

ANNA GODBERSEN

FAMILY IS NOT AN IMPORTANT THING. IT'S EVERYTHING.

MICHAEL J. FOX

> OUR SIBLINGS... RESEMBLE US JUST ENOUGH TO MAKE ALL THEIR DIFFERENCES CONFUSING... WE ARE CAST IN RELATION TO THEM OUR WHOLE LIVES LONG.
>
> Susan Scarf Merrell

NEVER BEND YOUR HEAD. ALWAYS HOLD IT HIGH. LOOK THE WORLD STRAIGHT IN THE EYE.

HELEN KELLER

> "We cannot destroy kindred: our chains stretch a little sometimes, but they never break."
>
> — Marquise de Sévigné

TO EACH OTHER, WE WERE AS NORMAL AND NICE AS THE SMELL OF BREAD. WE WERE JUST A FAMILY.

JOHN IRVING

You can be boring and tedious with sisters, whereas you have to put on a good face with friends.

Deborah Moggach

YOU KNOW
JUST HOW
TO MAKE
ME SMILE

FAMILIES... HUMANIZE YOU.
THEY ARE MADE TO MAKE
YOU FORGET YOURSELF
OCCASIONALLY, SO THAT THE
BEAUTIFUL BALANCE OF LIFE
IS NOT DESTROYED.

Anaïs Nin

> **HOW GOOD IT IS TO HAVE A SISTER WHOSE HEART IS AS YOUNG AS YOUR OWN.**
>
> Pam Brown

THE INFORMALITY OF FAMILY
LIFE IS A BLESSED CONDITION
THAT ALLOWS US ALL TO
BECOME OUR BEST WHILE
LOOKING OUR WORST.

Marge Kennedy

DON'T YOU EVER LET A SOUL IN THE WORLD TELL YOU THAT YOU CAN'T BE EXACTLY WHO YOU ARE.

LADY GAGA

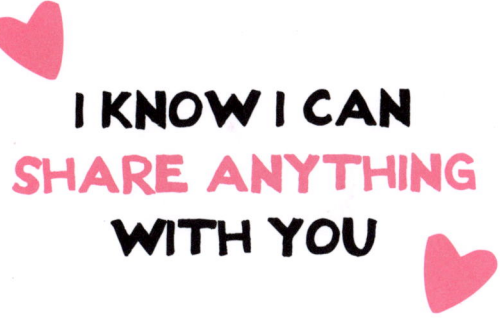

IN FAMILY LIFE, LOVE IS THE OIL THAT EASES FRICTION, THE CEMENT THAT BINDS... AND THE MUSIC THAT BRINGS HARMONY.

EVA BURROWS

Family life... etches itself into memory and personality. It's difficult to imagine anything more nourishing to the soul.

Thomas Moore

> MY SISTER TAUGHT ME EVERYTHING I REALLY NEED TO KNOW, AND SHE WAS ONLY IN SIXTH GRADE AT THE TIME.

Linda Sunshine

BE YOURSELF.
THE WORLD WORSHIPS THE ORIGINAL.

INGRID BERGMAN

Always remember, you have within you the strength, the patience, and the passion to reach for the stars, to change the world.

Harriet Tubman

FAMILY IS THE MOST IMPORTANT THING IN THE WORLD.

DIANA, PRINCESS OF WALES

SISTERS ARE DIFFERENT FLOWERS FROM THE SAME GARDEN

A SISTER IS ONE OF THE NICEST THINGS THAT CAN HAPPEN TO ANYONE.

Anonymous

RIDE THE ENERGY OF YOUR OWN **UNIQUE SPIRIT.**

Gabrielle Roth

SIBLING RELATIONSHIPS...
FLOURISH IN A THOUSAND
INCARNATIONS OF CLOSENESS
AND DISTANCE, WARMTH,
LOYALTY AND DISTRUST.

Erica E. Goode

NOTHING CAN DIM THE LIGHT WHICH SHINES FROM WITHIN.

MAYA ANGELOU

THERE IS NO TIME LIKE THE OLD TIME, WHEN YOU AND I WERE YOUNG!

OLIVER WENDELL HOLMES

YOU ARE MAGNIFICENT
BEYOND MEASURE, PERFECT
IN YOUR IMPERFECTIONS,
AND WONDERFULLY MADE.

Abiola Abrams

YOU KNOW ALL MY **SECRETS** AND **STILL** LOVE ME!

> "What greater thing is there for two human souls than to feel that they are joined for life... to be one with each other in silent unspeakable memories."
>
> George Eliot

DON'T LET THEM TAME YOU.

ISADORA DUNCAN

There is an interconnectedness among members that bonds the family, much like mountain climbers who rope themselves together when climbing.

Phil McGraw

> "THE STRENGTH OF A FAMILY, LIKE THE STRENGTH OF AN ARMY, LIES IN ITS *LOYALTY TO EACH OTHER*.

Mario Puzo

WHEN YOU LOOK AT YOUR LIFE, THE GREATEST HAPPINESSES ARE FAMILY HAPPINESSES.

Joyce Brothers

Have you enjoyed this book?
If so, find us on Facebook
at **Summersdale Publishers**,
on Twitter/X at **@Summersdale**
and on Instagram, TikTok and Bluesky at
@summersdalebooks and get in touch.
We'd love to hear from you!

www.summersdale.com

Image credits

p.1 – cover images © LizavetaS/Shutterstock.com and Bespana/Shutterstock.com

pp.4, 14, 16, 25, 27, 36, 38, 49, 51, 60, 62, 72, 75, 86, 90, 98, 100, 110, 112, 122, 124, 135, 137, 147, 149, 159 – decorations © Kathleen Johnson/Shutterstock.com

pp.5, 11, 17, 20, 26, 32, 39, 44, 50, 56, 63, 70, 77, 83, 88, 95, 101, 107, 113, 119, 125, 131, 136, 142, 148, 155, 158 – speech mark and line design © CkyBe/Shutterstock.com

pp.7, 9, 15, 21, 28, 33, 41, 45, 52, 57, 65, 68, 76, 81, 87, 92, 103, 106, 115, 118, 127, 130, 138, 143, 150, 153 – dots and lines © ninocka/Shutterstock.com

pp.13, 29, 42, 53, 64, 74, 84, 94, 105, 117, 129, 139, 154 – hearts Bespana/Shutterstock.com

WHEN YOU LOOK AT YOUR LIFE, THE GREATEST HAPPINESSES ARE FAMILY HAPPINESSES.

Joyce Brothers

Have you enjoyed this book?
If so, find us on Facebook
at **Summersdale Publishers**,
on Twitter/X at **@Summersdale**
and on Instagram, TikTok and Bluesky at
@summersdalebooks and get in touch.
We'd love to hear from you!

www.summersdale.com

Image credits

p.1 – cover images © LizavetaS/Shutterstock.com and Bespana/Shutterstock.com

pp.4, 14, 16, 25, 27, 36, 38, 49, 51, 60, 62, 72, 75, 86, 90, 98, 100, 110, 112, 122, 124, 135, 137, 147, 149, 159 – decorations © Kathleen Johnson/Shutterstock.com

pp.5, 11, 17, 20, 26, 32, 39, 44, 50, 56, 63, 70, 77, 83, 88, 95, 101, 107, 113, 119, 125, 131, 136, 142, 148, 155, 158 – speech mark and line design © CkyBe/Shutterstock.com

pp.7, 9, 15, 21, 28, 33, 41, 45, 52, 57, 65, 68, 76, 81, 87, 92, 103, 106, 115, 118, 127, 130, 138, 143, 150, 153 – dots and lines © ninocka/Shutterstock.com

pp.13, 29, 42, 53, 64, 74, 84, 94, 105, 117, 129, 139, 154 – hearts Bespana/Shutterstock.com